# Horseback Riding
## FOR FUN!

**By Beth Gruber**

*Content Adviser: Fiona L'Estrange, Federation Equestre Internationale Rider, Instructor, Stillwater, New Jersey*
*Reading Adviser: Frances J. Bonacci, Reading Specialist, Cambridge, Massachusetts*

**COMPASS POINT BOOKS**

**MINNEAPOLIS, MINNESOTA**

Compass Point Books
3109 West 50th Street, #115
Minneapolis, MN 55410

Visit Compass Point Books on the Internet at *www.compasspointbooks.com*
or e-mail your request to *custserv@compasspointbooks.com*

Photographs ©: Lisette Le Bon/SuperStock, front cover (left); PhotoDisc, front cover (top right), 11 (left), 42 (left and right); Comstock, front cover (bottom right); PhotoSpin, 4-5; Rubberball Productions, 7; Gabe Palmer/Corbis, 9; Corbis, 11 (right); Kit Houghton/Corbis, 13, 19, 27, 31, 39; Photos.com, 15 (left); Courtesy of Dover Saddlery, 15 (right), 16-17, 45 (bottom right); David Sacks/Getty Images, 25; SuperStock, 29; Al Bello/Allsport, 33; Richard A. Cooke/Corbis, 35; Gray Mortimore/Allsport, 37; Corel, 41, 42 (center), 43 (bottom right), 44 (left), 45 (bottom left), 47; Eyewire Images, 44 (right).

Editor: Sandra E. Will/Bill SMITH STUDIO
Photo Researchers: Sandra E. Will and Christie Silver/Bill SMITH STUDIO
Designer: Colleen Sweet and Brian Kobberger/Bill SMITH STUDIO

**Library of Congress Cataloging-in-Publication Data**
Gruber, Beth.
Horseback riding for fun / by Beth Gruber.
p. cm. — (Activities for fun)
Includes index.
Summary: An introduction to horseback riding, discussing a horse's anatomy, how to care for a horse, riding equipment and techniques, and various equestrian events.
ISBN 0-7565-0585-2 (hardcover)
ISBN 0-7565-1158-5 (paperback)
1. Horsemanship—Juvenile literature. [1. Horsemanship.] I. Title.
II. Series.
SF309.2.G78 2004
798.2'3—dc22

2003015821

# Table of Contents

## The Basics

## Doing It

## People, Places, and Fun

Note: In this book, there are two kinds of vocabulary words. Horseback Riding Words to Know are words specific to riding. They are in **bold** and are defined on page 46. Other Words to Know are helpful words that aren't related only to horseback riding. They are ***bold and italicized.*** These are defined on page 47.

# Horsing Around

**D**o you like horses? Horses have been around for a long, long time. In fact, the earliest horses were here on Earth at least 50 million years before the first human ever showed up!

The first horses were **_domesticated_** in Central Asia in about 4,500 B.C. Soon, people all over the world discovered how useful horses could be. For thousands of years, horse-drawn transportation was the only way to travel on land. Once people discovered just how smart and strong horses could be, farmers used them to help plow the land, turn the mills, and haul heavy equipment.

With the invention of the automobile, horses moved from crowded city streets to country farms. Here, riding and racing horses became popular sports.

Today, many people simply enjoy the pleasures of riding. Others train their horses for special events and compete in horse shows.

*Horses offer a world of fun for everyone.*

# Heads, Tails, and in Between

**H**orses come in different **breeds,** shapes, and sizes. Some, like the draft horse, are large and heavily built. Others, like the **thoroughbred,** are slender and fast. Ponies are smaller than traditional horses. They have shorter legs and are stronger in relation to their size.

When choosing a horse to ride, look at the horse's **conformation,** or overall body shape. Riding horses should be strong enough to carry someone on their backs but slender enough for you to straddle comfortably.

A horse's body parts are called **points.** Do you know any of the parts of a horse? Study the picture and learn the names of all the horse's points. You will need to know them when riding lessons begin.

crest

mane

poll

withers

forelock

dock

hindquarters

flank

thigh

stifle

hock

elbow

knee

forearm

cannon

heel

pastern

fetlock

hoof

7

# Making Friends

**M**ost people know the most basic rule about approaching a horse: never approach from the rear, or you could get kicked! To make friends with a horse, always approach from the front and at an angle. Talk to the horse in a calm voice as you get closer. Making friends with a horse is a lot like making friends with people. Start by building trust slowly. Ask the horse's owner or an instructor if the horse is shy, friendly, or likely to bite or kick. Learn to understand what a horse is saying.

Every horse has its own personality, just like humans do. Some are stubborn. Some are brave. Some are easily spooked. To tell what a horse is feeling, look at its ears and its face. An alert horse stands with both ears pointed forward. An angry horse will point its ears backward and flare its nostrils. Look out! A frightened horse will point its ears back, flare its nostrils, and roll its eyes until the white parts show. If this happens, get out of the way quickly. When a horse is excited, it will flare its nostrils, arch its neck, prick up its ears, and snort.

Find out from an instructor if the horse has been well-broken, or trained to carry a rider. This is especially important for riders who work with different horses when they are at the stable. A horse is a large and powerful animal that can harm a human if not treated properly.

*Building a good relationship with a horse takes time and patience, but it is worth it. Horses are loyal, affectionate, fun, and exciting.*

# Hard Work

**C**aring for a horse is fun. It is also hard and dirty work! Horses that live in a **stable** need a large, clean **stall,** lots of fresh food and water, and daily attention and exercise to stay happy and healthy.

A horse's stall must be cleaned, or mucked out, every single day. Use a pitchfork and a manure bucket or wheelbarrow to clean up the manure and wet **bedding.** To replace the bedding, spread fresh straw or wood shavings across the floor. Make a thick, soft layer at least 4 inches (10 centimeters) deep.

Horses need plenty of exercise, and they also need lots of fresh water: 8 to 12 gallons (30 to 40 liters) every day. They must be fed at least twice a day to stay healthy. In warm weather, horses can get their food on their own by **grazing** on grass. In winter months, they must be fed hay and **grain.**

Most riding schools have stable hands to tend to a horse's daily care. If you have time to make a large commitment, you will find that caring for horses is a great way to make friends with them.

For a special treat, try feeding a horse a carrot or an apple.

# Brush Up!

**E**ach horse reacts differently when being **groomed.** Some horses enjoy grooming so much that they fall asleep during the process. Others need to be tied with a quick-release knot or a **halter** to keep them still. All horses should be groomed every day.

When grooming a horse, you should make sure that an instructor tells you what to do. For safety, you should always make sure that an adult is present to supervise your work in the stable. Start with the top of the horse's head and work toward the **hindquarters.** Then, work down the legs. Do one side and then the other. Use firm, strong strokes.

Use a **dandy brush** with long, wiry bristles to remove dirt and sweat from the horse's coat. Use a **body brush** to smooth the horse's coat from head to tail. Use a mane comb to untangle the mane and tail. Soft sponges are perfect for cleaning a horse's eyes, mouth, nostrils, and dock (see p. 7). A hoof pick cleans all of the dirt from in between a horse's **hooves.**

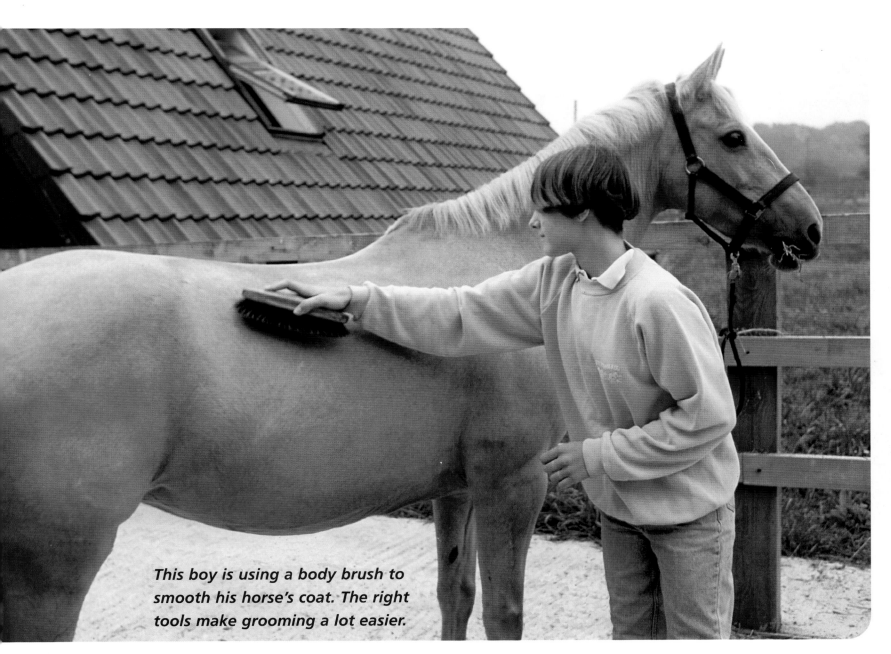

*This boy is using a body brush to smooth his horse's coat. The right tools make grooming a lot easier.*

# Tack It On

Grooming equipment isn't the only equipment a rider needs. **Tack** is the word used to describe the equipment a horse wears when someone rides it. The most basic pieces of tack are the bridle and the saddle.

The bridle has a set of soft leather straps that fasten around a horse's head and a **bit** that goes into the horse's mouth. The bit is held in place by more leather straps that attach to the **reins.** Riders use reins, along with natural aids (see p. 24), to steer or guide a horse.

A saddle is a seat that rests on the horse's back. It is usually made from wood and metal and covered with padding and leather. A saddle helps protect the horse's spine. It also helps riders balance securely on a horse's back.

There are two kinds of saddles—English and Western. English saddles are used for jumping, hunting, and showing. Western saddles are used for ranching, pleasure-class riding, and rodeo. They are heavier than English saddles, have a deeper seat, and a high back. They also have a horn at the front for attaching rope.

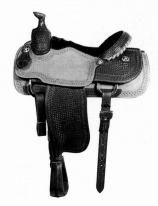

**English Saddle**     **Western Saddle**

# Sitting Pretty

**U**nlike some activities, horseback riding does not require a lot of special equipment. Beginning riders need sturdy boots with a low heel, comfortable pants, good gloves, and a protective helmet to get started.

Riders choose riding boots in black or brown leather with a smooth sole and a small heel. Most beginners wear boots that reach just above the ankle. Knee-length boots are used mainly for special occasions or horse shows.

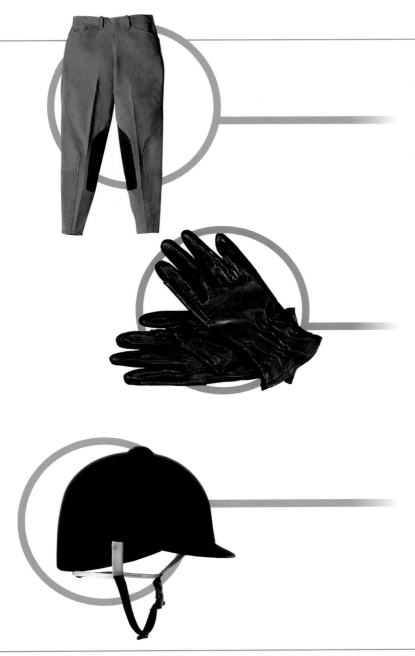

When selecting pants, horseback riders look for ones that let them move easily. **Jodhpurs** were especially designed for riders. They are made of stretchy fabric and are padded at the knee to prevent saddle rubs.

Riding gloves can be made of wool, cotton, or leather. They should have grips on the palms and fingers for holding on to the reins.

It is important to wear an approved helmet for safety. Helmets protect riders' heads in case they fall or are thrown from the horse. Riding helmets should fit snugly enough to stay in place, even when a rider bends over. They should have a chin strap and a thick layer of padding inside.

# You and Your Horse

**L**earning how to ride takes time, training, and commitment. The best place to start is at a riding school. Kids can start taking lessons as young as 5 or 6 years old. A well-run riding school will have neat stables, happy horses, a clean muck heap, and up-to-date equipment available for sale or rental. Look for a school that has qualified instructors, small classes, and horses that are suitable for beginners. Check to see if there is an indoor riding ring for schooling, or **flatwork.** Schooling is the method used to train a horse to be balanced and well-behaved. Good schooling will help both the horse and the rider.

Riding schools can be large or small. To find a good riding school in your area, check with the Pony Club. Find a school with students your age that is recognized by a riding organization. Then, take a lesson.

*It can take many lessons to learn how to ride. Some schools offer free or discounted lessons in return for helping out around the barn.*

# On and Off

**A**re you ready to ride? First, you need to learn how to saddle up. Be sure you have an instructor nearby to supervise and assist. Begin by placing a **saddle pad** or blanket on the horse's back. Next, pick up the saddle. Hold the **pommel** of the saddle with your left hand. Then, place your right hand under the seat. Put the right **stirrup** over the seat so it does not get caught when you swing the saddle onto the back of the horse. Next, stand near the horse's left side and place the saddle gently on the horse's back. Then, reach under the horse's belly to let down the **girth** and tighten it under the horse's elbows. Finally, lower the stirrups until they hang approximately an arm's length from the saddle.

To mount, or get on, a horse, stand near the horse's left side. Take the reins in your left hand and hold the pommel. Place your left foot in the stirrup iron. Stand on a mounting box if you are not tall enough to reach the stirrup.

Next, hold the **cantle** and step up. Swing your right leg over the back of the saddle and lower yourself gently down until you are sitting comfortably. Finally, place your right foot in the stirrup.

1

2

3

To dismount, wait until the horse is standing still. Take both feet out of the stirrups and lean forward. Then, swing your right leg back and over the saddle. Lower yourself down and land on both feet. Remember to hold the reins in case the horse moves.

# Take Your Seat

**A**re you comfortable sitting on the horse? An accomplished rider can sit securely in the saddle without holding on to the reins. This is called having an "independent seat." To develop an independent seat, sit in the center of the saddle and place both feet in the stirrups. Keep your head up, your back straight, and your heels down.

Now, ask an instructor to hold the horse while you try these exercises:

Keep both feet in the stirrups and lean back as far as possible. Then, try leaning forward. Keep both legs straight down.

How comfortable are you? Can you touch your toes? It's not so easy when you're sitting on a horse! Keep both legs in the stirrups and try to reach your left hand across the horse and touch your right foot. Then, reverse and try it the other way.

Next, try standing up! Keep your feet in the stirrups with your weight on your heels. Lift up out of the saddle and hold your arms out to your sides for balance.

Finally, sit back down in the saddle. Remove both feet from the stirrups and raise them out to the sides. Extend both of your arms as well.

Practice these exercises and you'll develop an independent seat quickly.

# Ready, Set, Ride

**O**nce you can saddle a horse, mount and dismount, and maintain an independent seat, you are ready to ride!

Use natural aids, such as your hands, legs, voice, and seat, to let a horse know what it is supposed to do. To get going, gently press both legs against the horse's sides. To turn right, shift your weight slightly to the right and squeeze the horse's left side gently with your heel and calf. At the same time, squeeze the right rein. Reverse the movement to turn the horse left.

When you want the horse to move forward, make a clicking sound with your mouth, and use a voice command like "walk."

To stop, apply gentle pressure on both reins at the same time. Keep your weight deep in the saddle and your shoulders, hips, and heels in a straight line. Use the voice command "whoa" to *reinforce* the movement.

# Walking and Trotting

**F**ast or slow? How will you go? Humans have two legs that they use to walk or run. Horses have four legs, and they have four different ways of moving: walk, trot, **canter,** and gallop. The way a horse moves is called a **gait.**

The slowest gait is the walk. When a horse walks, it moves from one hindleg to the foreleg on one side, then from the opposite hindleg to the foreleg on the other side. Listen to hear the steady one-two-three-four beat as the horse's hooves hit the ground. You should keep your body still when the horse is walking, except for a slight movement at the hips and waist. Your hands should give, or move, slightly as the horse nods its head.

Trotting is a horse's most natural gait. When a horse trots, it springs **diagonally** from one pair of legs to the other. To make the change from walking to trotting, use both of your legs to squeeze the horse's sides. Go up on the first beat of the trot and come down on the second. This is called posting. It takes a little while to get used to posting because the beat of the horse will feel unnatural at first.

*You can tell a horse's gait by listening to the number of beats that it makes. The diagonal movement of the trot creates two beats.*

# Cantering and Galloping

**A**re you ready to pick up the pace? It is best to practice in a fenced ring first. Otherwise, you could wind up on a runaway horse!

To make a horse move from a trot to a canter, stop posting. Then, apply inside leg pressure on the girth and outside leg pressure behind the girth. Squeeze the inside rein until the horse begins to canter. Then, release it. Listen for the beat of the horse's hooves as one hindleg, then the other, and then the forelegs strike the ground. Listen for the moment of silence when the horse's feet are completely off the ground. Sit down in the saddle for all three beats. Hold on to the horse with both of your legs to avoid bouncing around in the saddle, which makes you and the horse uncomfortable.

*Race horses use the gallop to speed around the track. You can tell if a horse is galloping by counting the beats. A gallop has four beats.*

The gallop is the horse's fastest gait. To change from canter to gallop, squeeze the horse's sides with the lower part of the legs and sit up and forward in the saddle. Then, bend forward at the waist and move both hands slightly up the horse's neck. Hold the reins firmly but make sure that you do not pull back on the reins. Pulling back on the reins will tell a horse to stop instead of go!

# Up and Over

**J**umping comes naturally to most horses. Still, it takes a lot of practice for a horse and rider to learn to jump together safely. Be sure to work with an experienced horse and a good instructor when you're learning.

Do not be surprised if the first jumps you learn are very small. To practice, place a series of evenly spaced poles on the ground. Walk, then trot, the horse over the poles. Next, leave the first pole on the ground and raise the second pole slightly. Finally, try raising both poles off the ground. As you improve, your teacher will gradually raise the height of the poles.

There are five steps to every jump:

1. During the "approach," bend forward slightly and look straight ahead.

2. As you and your horse "take off," squeeze both legs against the horse's sides. Bend all the way forward.

3. In flight, balance your weight over the saddle. Lift your seat out of the saddle and bend forward at the waist.

4. Give the horse as much rein as it needs during "landing," but do not drop the reins. Otherwise, the horse might trip and fall. Return to an upright seat. Take up the reins again only after the horse has landed.

5. To make a clean "getaway," maintain an upright seat and ride away from the jump. Continue to look straight ahead.

# The Big Events

Local horse shows allow riders to perfect their skills and prepare for more challenging competitions. It takes years of practice for a rider and horse to compete in big international events, but anyone can compete in a horse show. Horse shows offer year-round opportunities for riders of every age and skill level to compete and have fun in a variety of different events.

The Summer Olympic Games and the World Championships are the world's toughest **equestrian** competitions. The Olympics are held every four years, and the World Championships take place every year. At these events, the top riders from around the world come to compete. They participate in both individual and team events.

Young riders at the top of their class compete in Junior Olympic Equestrian Events. These events provide excellent preparation for the Summer Olympics and the World Championships.

Jeanette Brakewell of Great Britain competes in the Three Day Show Jumping event at the 2000 Summer Olympic Games.

# Beginners' Competitions

**G**ymkhana games are ideal competitions for beginning riders. Each game tests a particular skill of the horse and rider as a team.

*Precision* games test a horse and rider's *accuracy* and *agility.* Can you sit *astride* a horse and balance a ball on a cone while the horse walks? Can you guide a horse along a line of stepping stones without falling out of step? Small, obedient horses are often the best at these games. Accuracy, not speed, is what counts here.

Speed games test how fast a horse and rider can go. Can you ride a horse in and out of a line of barrels? Can you do it quickly without knocking down any barrels? You'll need to finish ahead of all the other riders to win a speed game.

Mixed games test both precision and skill. Practice both, and you'll be ready for the toughest competition!

Once you have mastered the beginner level, you can ride in more advanced events. Some young riders move on to compete in rodeos.

*A child competes in a barrel racing event.*

# Take Control

**T**he most popular events at an English-style horse show take place inside and outside the ring. **Show jumping** and **hunter events** are held inside the ring. For these events, the ring is laid out with *obstacles* which the horse must jump over in order. When a horse knocks down an obstacle, it counts as a fault, or penalty. The best jumpers are the riders who can guide their horses around the course in the shortest time, with the fewest faults.

Speed and endurance events take place outside the ring, over miles of trails, roads, and hills. Horses and their riders *navigate* uneven ground and take challenging jumps.

At a Western show, riders have a chance to shine in classes, such as pole bending, barrels, keyhole, speed, and flags. Like hunter events, these classes judge a horse and rider on how quickly and accurately they can navigate an obstacle course. Other classes, including the Western Pleasure class, judge a horse and rider on how well they carry themselves.

*Riders compete in the show jumping event at the International Horse Show in London, England, which is an English-style show held every year.*

# Perfect Paces

**D**ressage means training, and that is exactly what a horse and rider need to master to bring home a dressage ribbon. Each dressage event consists of a series of tests that are performed in an arena. The tests last about five minutes and include a variety of movements and paces, such as the half-pass and the pirouette. In the half-pass, dressage riders move their horses forward and sideways. The more difficult the move, the more riders move their horses sideways. Dressage riders canter their horses in a circle on the spot to create a pirouette.

Riders and their horses are graded on overall performance with marks ranging from one to 10. Judges may also include comments with their scores. The rider with the highest marks wins. Practice, practice, and more practice is the key to doing well in dressage events.

*These dressage riders are coming around the corner and preparing to perform their next movement.*

# Racing and Rodeos

**P**eople love to watch horses perform in races and at the rodeo. Horse racing is an international sport. The best riders, called jockeys, and horses compete in events all over the world. Some of the most famous horse races are the English Derby, the Kentucky Derby, and the Australian Melbourne Cup. One of the highest honors a racing horse can win is called the Triple Crown. To win the Crown, a horse must win three major races in the same year: the Kentucky Derby, the Preakness, and the Belmont Stakes. Only 11 horses have ever won the Triple Crown.

At rodeos, cowboys and cowgirls rope calves while riding on the back of a horse. The rider with the fastest time wins. Cowboys also try to stay on horses while they buck up and down. The rider who can stay on the horse for the longest period of time without being thrown off wins!

Whether you visit the race track, the rodeo, or your local stable, horseback riding has something fun for everyone.

Rodeos are popular in many regions of the United States and Canada. Some rodeos have competitions for riders as young as 8 years old.

# What Happened When?

| 400 B.C. | 365 A.D. | 600-1000 | 1381 | 1493-1519 | 1700 | 1806 | 1860 |

**400 B.C.** Xenophon, a Greek soldier and author, writes the first manual on horseback riding. He calls it "The Art of Horsemanship."

**365 A.D.** The first Western saddle is invented by the Sarmatians, a tribe living in what is now southern Russia.

**600–1000** Advances in saddle development make it possible for horses to be used for leisure riding, tournaments, carrying messages, and war.

**1381** Anne of Bohemia, wife of England's King Richard II, introduces sidesaddle riding for women.

**1493–1519** Spanish explorers Christopher Columbus and Hernán Cortés reintroduce the horse in North America. Native Americans who have never seen a horse before are terrified.

**1700s** The Conestoga wagon becomes a symbol of the pioneer spirit. It is pulled by horses.

**1806** William D. Davis applies for and receives a patent for a horseback riding saddle.

**1867** The first Belmont Stakes race is run.

**1870** The first Preakness is run at Pimlico Race Course in Maryland.

**1872** T. J. Byrd applies for and receives a patent for a horse yoke device, a horse and carriage device, and horse reins.

**1873** The North West Mounted Police is commissioned. Their horses are trained for police work.

**1875** The first Kentucky Derby is held at Churchill Downs in Louisville, Kentucky. The winner is a horse named Aristedes.

**1880**    **1900**    **1920**    **1940**    **1960**    **1980**    **2000**

**1886** Cowboys and their horses compete publicly in a sport that comes to be known as the rodeo.

**1900** Show jumping is the first equestrian event to be recognized as an Olympic sport.

**1908** Cars begin to replace horse-drawn transportation when Henry Ford starts producing automobiles.

**1914–1918** The horse is used to carry soldiers and transport equipment during World War I. More than 375,000 horses are killed in battle. This is the last major war in which horses were used. By World War II, horses are replaced with vehicles.

**1919** Sir Barton becomes the first race horse to win the Triple Crown.

**1937** USA Equestrian founds the Equitation Medal program to recognize junior riders who display outstanding skill in the saddle.

**1938** Seabiscuit is voted Horse of the Year for his dominance in the racing world.

**1954** The United States Pony Club is founded.

**1969** The North American Riding for the Handicapped Association is established for people with disabilities.

**1977** Seattle Slew wins the Triple Crown.

**1988** The Special Olympics add riding as a competitive sport.

**1990** The first World Equestrian Games are held in Stockholm, Sweden.

**2002** The World Equestrian Games in Jerez de la Frontera, Spain, is the largest organized equestrian event ever. Fifty-three nations compete for seven world championships.

**2003** The movie "Seabiscuit," starring Tobey Maguire and Jeff Bridges, is released and becomes a big hit.

**43**

# Horseback Riding Highlights

The height of a horse is measured in hands. One hand is equal to 4 inches (10.2 centimeters). The tallest horse ever recorded stood 21.25 hands high and weighed 2,976 pounds (1,351 kilograms). His name was Firpon. Brooklyn Supreme was the world's heaviest horse, topping the scales at 3,174 pounds (1,441 kg).

Did you know that most horses have brown eyes? A horse's eyes are usually dark, like the color of a horse's skin. Only spotted horses, albino horses, and certain other breeds have light-colored eyes.

Do spots and stripes really go together? They do in the horse world. Most horses with spotted coats have striped hooves.

Why do horses sleep standing up? It is something horses learned to do in the wild to help them make a fast escape. Today, most domesticated horses still sleep standing up. It is a natural instinct!

Who would have believed that a knobby-kneed horse named Seabiscuit would become one of the most famous horses of all time? This spirited little horse captured the hearts of Americans during the 1930s by shattering speed records and winning more races than any other horse during his time!

Horses usually give birth at night. Why? It is the time when a herd is least likely to be on the move.

**Whips** and **spurs** are artificial aids. They are only used by the most experienced riders. Each of these will urge a horse to move forward. Neither should ever be used to hurt a horse.

# Horseback Riding Words to Know

**bedding:** a blanket of straw or wood shavings that covers the floor in a horse's stall

**bit:** the metal part of the bridle that goes in a horse's mouth

**body brush:** a soft brush used to smooth a horse's coat; usually made of horsehair

**breed:** groups or families of horses that share the same features, such as color and height

**canter:** a horse's fast, bounding pace

**cantle:** the back part of a saddle

**conformation:** a horse's overall appearance

**dandy brush:** a brush with long, wiry bristles

**dressage:** an elegant equestrian sport that tests the performance and style of a horse and rider, as well as the horse's obedience

**equestrian:** about or relating to horseback riding; also someone who rides on horseback

**flatwork:** a system for training a horse to perform basic paces; also called schooling

**gait:** the manner in which a horse moves

**girth:** the distance around a horse when measured from behind the withers

**grain:** concentrated food; has more food content than what a horse eats naturally from the land

**grazing:** the manner in which a horse nibbles on grass

**grooming:** brushing and cleaning a horse

**gymkhana:** games or races performed on horseback

**halter:** a piece of tack used on a horse's head for catching, leading, or tying up

**hindquarters:** the half of a horse's body located behind the saddle area

**hoof:** the hard covering that encloses a horse's foot

**hunter event:** a class that tests a rider's ability to control and maneuver a horse around obstacles in a ring

**jodhpurs:** pants specially designed for horseback riding

**points:** the different parts of a horse

**pommel:** a knob at the top front part of a Western saddle

**reins:** leather straps that are attached to the bit and held in a rider's hand

**saddle pad:** a piece of cloth that goes between the saddle and a horse's back to prevent rubbing

**show jumping:** a jumping class that takes place in an arena at an event

**spurs:** metal spokes that go around the back of a rider's boot and are used to move a horse forward

**stable:** a building or barn where horses are kept

**stall:** the partially enclosed area in a stable where a horse lives

**stirrups:** the part of a saddle where riders put their feet

**tack:** the gear needed to ride a horse, including the saddle and the bridle

**thoroughbred:** a purebred horse

**whip:** an artificial aid made of leather used to urge a horse forward

# Other Words to Know

Here are definitions for some of the words used in this book:

**accuracy:** the quality of being exact

**agility:** the ability to move in a quick and easy way

**astride:** with one leg on each side

**diagonally:** moving from front to back on opposite sides in a criss-cross fashion

**domesticated:** tamed for use by humans

**navigate:** to steer a course

**obstacle:** an object that makes it difficult to move in one direction or another

**precision:** moving in an exact manner

**reinforce:** to strengthen with additional materials

## Where to Learn More

### AT THE LIBRARY

Budd, Jackie. *Horses*. New York: Larousse Kingfisher Chambers, Inc., 2001.

Clader, Kate. *Horseback Riding in Action*. New York: Crabtree Publishing Company, 2001.

Webber, Toni. *Me and My Horse*. Brookfield, Conn.: Copper Beech Books, 2002.

### ON THE ROAD

Bitterroot Dude Ranch
1480 E. Fork Road
Dubois, WY 82513
800/545-0019
www.bitterrootranch.com

**Kentucky Horse Park and International Museum of the Horse**
4089 Iron Works Parkway
Lexington, KY 40511
800/678-8813
www.imh.org

### ON THE WEB

For more information on *horseback riding,* use FactHound to track down Web sites related to this book.

1. Go to www.compasspointbooks.com/facthound
2. Type in this book ID: 0756505852
3. Click on the *FETCH IT* button.

Your trusty FactHound will fetch the best Web sites for you!

# INDEX

## ABOUT THE AUTHOR

Beth Gruber has worked in children's book publishing for almost 20 years as an author, editor, and reviewer of many books for young readers. She also interviews other authors and TV show creators who write for children. Beth is a graduate of NYU School of Journalism. Reading and writing are her passions. She lives in New York City.